Being You Through the Noise

MELISSA MIFSUD

Copyright © 2023 Melissa Mifsud
Melbourne, Australia
All rights reserved.

ISBN: 978-0-6457897-0-6
Imprint: Independently Published

The content of this book is for informational purposes only and not to be substituted for professional advice. By reading this book you are thereby agreeing to take full responsibility for any actions you choose to take from the information provided.

Dedication

To the young girl who was lost, who felt like she needed others to love and fulfill her. This book is for you, it's your reminder that you don't need anyone to create your own happiness.

Preface	7
Introduction	9
Chapter one: Childhood Traumas and Triggers	13
Chapter two: Hello Inner Child	45
Chapter three: Discovering who you are	63
Chapter four: Who are you in your relationships?	87
Chapter five: Don't get lost in the external world	101
Chapter six: The happy-self	113
With thanks	123
References	125
Acknowledgments	127
About the author	129

Preface

Growing up I always had a passion for reading and writing. My mum would always buy me new stationery that I asked for, even though she thought I already had too much. I would always be in my bedroom with a piece of A4 white paper stuck on my cupboard with blue tack pretending to teach my imaginary group of children. Since fulfilling my childhood dream of becoming a qualified early childhood teacher, I have spent many hours in the classroom sharing my passion with many children.

Becoming a teacher revealed much more to me than just how to share my passion and teach children. What I learnt through my experience was how to find the spark for my own journey of self-love and personal growth. And from this, I know I am meant to share my journey and what I have discovered with the world.

While teaching in my third year out of university, I met a lady called Elly. Elly is a wise experienced teacher who supported me in the classroom while teaching. Elly provided me with a different perspective on life at the time and this was when I had my turning point and realised I had to do the inner work. It allowed me to use what I had learnt with what I had been, putting them together, to awaken me within my teaching practices. Especially because I taught 3-5-year old's and saw clearly just how crucial the first five years of a child's life is.

I was born to do this; I was born to use my voice and share it, but first I had to discover who I was, I had to ignite my self-confidence, and break through those self-doubts. Here I am now, and here you are now about to embark on a wonderful journey of your own as you read through this book.

While writing this book it took me on another journey, a journey of realisation, realising how far I've come and how excited I am to share with you what I've learnt.

My hope for you is that by immersing in my story and my realisations along the way, that you feel more yourself than ever before.

I begin this book with an open heart

In the past I may have said incomplete, but the truth is I was wounded. I spent many years finding love in men, finding myself in relationships, and finding myself putting others needs and wants before my own. Going through the experiences of not feeling good enough, not loving who I was, not knowing how to say 'no' to others, and not seeing the true beauty I had within, allowed me to discover; self-acceptance, self- worth, and most of all, self-love. I still sit here with a heavy and grateful heart as I've experienced the crucial times of growing up without having a stable father figure, however, I still feel very grateful that I now get to spend time with my dad.

I know that starting a book with discovering how the influences from your childhood has played a significant part in who you are today may seem daunting, however, I want you to know that I'll be here with you every step of the way.

Does part of you just want to skip the part where all the hard work is done and everything will be all good with a click of a finger? I sure did, but that wouldn't be as fun. We wouldn't grow and learn into the conscious human beings we are meant to be. I wrote this book as I could see the power of discovering who I am to the core and I want to share with you how you can use that to create magic.

This book isn't just going to guide you, it's going to support you in becoming more of yourself than ever before. It's going to ensure you can hold yourself through those challenging times and allow you to choose the life you want to create.

It's about finding what sets your inner child on fire and allowing you to embrace every moment, which we will dive deeper into a little later in this book. I remember feeling happy and free when I would ride my bike or just be outside embracing what nature has to offer. It's those simple things we seem to take for granted but yet give us the most excitement.

We all have a story to tell, and while everyone's story is different, I feel we can all resonate with not doing enough for ourselves.

Take what you feel resonates and enjoy.

Melissa xx

One ♡
Childhood Traumas and Triggers

I was a young, quiet, friendly, adventurous, and bubbly girl that had a great childhood. I remember it so clearly, throughout the summer days my siblings and I would be out the front of our family home with our neighbours eating Zooper Doopers, riding our bikes, rolling our roller blades, or playing tiggy. And in the winter days my siblings and I would be cosy at home playing Lego shops. We would build our own items to sell in our shop out of Lego and purchase off one another with 'Lego money,' or we would be trying to figure out which DVD to watch. As you may know back in the day having a copy of every favourite movie on DVD was a must have.

My mum and dad divorced when I was four years old. I was still quite young, but not young enough to not know and feel what was happening. I remember feeling sad, helpless, frustrated, and defeated in which I still have some very clear memories of events that took place when I was months old, yep only months old, that still haven't left my mind. Memories of being held in a capsule, when mum was walking through the hallway leaving the house as dad and her just had a disagreement. I remember crying as I could feel the intensity of their energy.

If there is one thing that has been highlighted to me throughout my journey, it's that our childhood shapes us into the person we become as an adult. My mother used to always say to my siblings and I 'children are a product of their environment.' I never quite understood what she meant until I did the inner work myself and discovered a lot about who I am today and how it links to my childhood.

The brains of infants and young children are always "on," taking in and processing stimuli from the people in their lives and surrounding environment. In an article written by internationally recognised experts in brain-based teaching, Donna Wilson and Marcus Conyers, that focused on how children flourished in the first five years. They explored the importance of the child's brain development in those early years. In the article they researched a study that states the brain is "the most immature of all organs at birth" they go on to say "it grows and develops based on an infant's interactions with people and objects around him or her".

A child learns from the influences within their environment in which invariably shapes them into the person that they become.

Different influences can be:

- Parenting styles such as: permissive, strict, neglectful, and gentle. How each child is raised to communicate and relate to others, as well as how they respond to other external influences can be largely influenced by the parenting style they grew up with and how their parent responds to the child during a certain situation. For example: learning how to communicate to others. While different parenting styles may have an influence it's also to not place 'blame' onto the parent who was doing the best they could at that time.

- Siblings. How a person interacts with their siblings can have an influence on how they respond to their outer world as each sibling has a different personality and traits. Someone who grew up as an only child, or grew up with siblings that have a large age gap would be influenced differently within their family environment.

- Extended family. A person's place within their family dynamics and culture will influence their personality.

- Influenced by friends. Being around friends who are gentle, kind, and caring will have an influence on how a person responds to those around them. Being in a friendship group that has a different dynamic offers a different experience that may not always be positive.

- Environment of where you live, where you go to rest and recharge, and where you go to hang out with your friends, as well as any other place you spend a lot of time growing up.

We are all born with some core traits that shine through regardless of the life we live and the environment we have grown up in. The two same people that live in the same house and have experienced the same life with their parents and siblings could still be different because of who they are internally. It is our childhood experiences along with who we are that innately shape us as adults.

All these influences mentioned above are things we are born into as a child. We don't get to choose many of our childhood experiences, just like we don't get to choose the school our parents send us too. These influences shape us by decisions we didn't get to make ourselves. However, now as adults we're able to take responsibility and are able to be in control of how we chose to live our life, who our circle of friends are, and the environments we chose to be in.

Reflecting as an adult, and as an educator, it has highlighted the importance of the first five years of our life and the influence those years have on the person we live as, as adults.

Let's take a moment to think about your memories as a child?

How do those memories make you feel?

How have those memories shaped you?

Growing up I was always close to my mum. Mum was the one who did everything for me, from bathing me to changing me, to providing me lunch orders at school, to being there at my parent teacher interviews, and to being the only one I could trust and open up too. This meant for a lot of my younger years while growing up that my dad was in and out of my life. I didn't have a stable male figure to show me how much I meant to him and/or guide me throughout situations where I felt a male's perspective was needed. My older brother did the best he could but a 10-year-old trying to fill that role of a father is just different.

My childhood was shaped by spending time with my mum, whereas my experience would've been different if it was the opposite.

Growing up I was in and out of relationships just like my dad was in and out of my life. I would never be single for too long, as I would start talking to a guy and would latch onto him straight away. It reached the point where this continually happened until I was 25 years old and met a new guy- let's call him Josh. I saw bright red flags from the beginning but still continued to pursue what we had, as I felt like I needed to 'feel loved by a man' in order to be happy and complete. I didn't realise what I was doing at the time, I only saw the pattern of being in and out of relationships later in life as I reflected back.

I did know that Josh wasn't the one for me but I still hung in there. Bizarre right!? I know what you're thinking, how could a person know the relationship they're in isn't healthy, but still stay in it, and reflecting back I'm wondering the same thing too. As I didn't receive stable love from a male figure, I tended to latch onto those I got into relationships with, as they were what made me feel 'safe, happy, and loved'. When a person gave me that feeling, I replaced it with everything that's happened.

Reflecting on the repeated behaviour of being in and out of relationships allowed me to see how the trauma played out in my life when growing up. Think back to your childhood and ask yourself these questions, and see if you can discover what your childhood triggers and traumas may look like.

- What situations or patterns seem to keep repeating in my life?
- What from your childhood could have influenced these behaviours and patterns?

Having childhood triggers and traumas doesn't take away the good times we've experienced when growing up, it just means there is duality within our experience.

In order to move through our triggers and traumas we need to recgonise what it looks and feels like. Adults who are healing from childhood trauma usually learn to interact with others in unhealthy ways. A few examples of unhealthy behaviours are: 'lying,' not being able to say 'no' because they are afraid of fear and rejection, and relying on other people's opinions, feelings and ideas more than their own.

Having unhealed trauma can appear differently in all of us. Having a low sense of self-worth can look like putting others needs and wants before your own and sacrificing yourself for others. Relying on the other person in the relationship where you're not able to make decisions and choices for yourself. Fear of being abandoned, as you believe you have to stay with a person because you don't want to be alone. Needing external validation, because you have self-doubt and don't see the beauty in you. Being afraid of what happens next, because the unknown is too scary. Agreeing to anything and everything because you're a people pleaser and will make sure other people are happy before you are. You will be in toxic relationships because as long as you're making the other person happy that's all that matters, right?

Though, no matter what experience you encounter you have taken the first step in becoming aware of unhealed trauma, and the rest of the book provides more guidance that will support you to begin moving through it.

Trauma.
/trau-ma/noun

(1) An emotional response to an event, often having long-lasting mental effects; (2) any physical damage to the body caused by emotional distress.

Unhealed trauma can look like:

- Low sense of self worth
- Over-relying on the other person in a relationship
- Fear of being abandoned
- Putting aside your needs for other people
- Needing external validation
- Always afraid of what might happen next
- Tolerating unacceptable behaviour from others
- Agreeing to anything and everything
- Being in toxic relationships
- Difficulty trusting others
- Difficulty setting clear boundaries

Throughout my relationship with Josh, I discovered that I relied on him to be the source of my happiness. I used to drop everything and anything for him, just so I could be with him. I would sacrifice so much of myself just to make him happy. Josh would be the reason why I was happy, sad, angry, frustrated, or annoyed. I looked for everything I needed in me, in him. I've always described it as 'I had a hole in my heart and I used him to fill it'.

You may be wondering how this links to my childhood. I myself didn't have the answer to that until two and a half years ago when one day Josh decided we should go couples counselling. Still to this day, that's the only counselling I have been to and it was the best thing I ever agreed to doing with Josh. Being open and raw to a counsellor felt daunting at first, but knowing they were there to support me was reassuring.

Throughout couples counselling, our counsellor helped me discover a lot about why I was reacting to situations the way I was. I remember us sitting in the room by ourselves and her telling me "you have an anxious attachment style and the reason for that is because your dad abandoned you when you were a child." At that point I was just like 'wow,' I was speechless, but from that moment it all slowly started coming together for me. From having this conversation with my counsellor, it allowed me to realise that I couldn't change him. I couldn't have him the way I wanted him to be.

This was my experience and through this relationship I was able to see the contrast to the love I wanted and the way I was being treated. When you look at your own relationships or experiences in life- what is contradicting?

During my relationship with Josh, we would always have our happy moments which wouldn't last too long as we would always find ourselves in sticky situations where a lot of disagreements occurred. It ended up being an unhealthy toxic relationship for nearly two years. I'll explain more about relationships later on in this book, but there is one thing I do want you to know now - relationships, whether it is friendships, or having an intimate partner, is a two-way street. One person cannot be the only one carrying the team on their back, because eventually they're going to get tired.

Going to couples counselling allowed me to think of different ways I could help strengthen my relationship with Josh, as at this point it wasn't about me, it was all about him and my relationship with him.
It was an average day relaxing on the couch, one cold day at Josh's house scrolling through Instagram, when I came across a

post from Chloe Szep about the 'Bloom app' she created. If you follow or know of Chloe you will know she is very spiritual and understands/shares the importance of self-care. When I saw the photo of Chloe announcing the launch of her 'Bloom app' I decided to click onto the tag and explore the Bloom Instagram page. Everything about the page, the words, the pictures, everything, you name it, caught my attention. I was intrigued to see what it was all about. Before I knew it, I signed up for a fourteen-day free trial. Through this app I discovered meditation and started to do meditations in the app with Josh. Little did Josh know that while meditating with him I was building my self-awareness and confidence to realise the relationship I wanted and that he did not match that ambition.

Meditation allows you to be present, while allowing you to break through your subconscious mind as you enter into a deep relaxing conscious state. For example: guided meditation taught me acceptance. It taught me that I had to accept whatever the situation may be because if I didn't, I would get angry, annoyed, and frustrated only to still not have control of the situation.

My meditation practice taught me that I didn't always need to have control of situations and didn't need to know the end results. Which I know is a big thing for a lot of us. As humans we tend to feel the need to be in control, we feel the need to know what's going to happen next or else we can't handle it… why? Why do we feel the need to be in control? What does being in control prove? How does it make us feel when we're in control? Is it our ego?

Once you learn to accept things for what they are, you begin to create a happier life for yourself as you have no 'expectation' on what the outcome will be. As Dr. Joe Dispenza says "meditation opens the door between the conscious and subconscious minds. We meditate to enter the operating system of the subconscious, where all of those unwanted habits and behaviours reside, and change them to more productive modes to support us in our lives."

Your relationships with family, friends, or your partner has many different details to mine, consider how your relationships impact you?

Take this moment to think about your top five relationships with those you either spend the most time with or people that you're close to.

Trigger.
/tri-gr/ noun

A stimulus that elicits a reaction. For example: an event could be a trigger for a memory of a past experience and an accompanying state of emotional arousal.

As a qualified early childhood teacher, I taught kindergarten for four years when one day I was working in the room with a lady called 'Elly.' I didn't know much about Elly even though we worked in the room together a handful of times before, we only really spoke about work. One day something drew me to open up about my relationship with Josh. I followed my intuition (which I didn't know I was doing at the time) and asked Elly for her advice on what I should do with a situation I was experiencing. To my surprise she opened me up to a whole new different perspective on life, that's right, not the relationship... **life.** Let me tell you why.

Through the many conversations Elly and I subsequently had about my ex and talking through the challenges I was bringing up; her core piece of advice would always lead back to: being present. From this, I had realised that when I am conscious and present, I'm able to think clearly in the moment.

When you are conscious throughout every moment in your life, whether it's through conversations or interactions with others, you're able to navigate whatever you may be experiencing with a higher degree of clarity. This is because your thoughts aren't driving you into trying to predict the future, or remembering what's happened in the past. Though, when you're present in the moment, everything is clear and that's why all my conversations with Elly led back to 'be present.' As when you're over thinking and analysing situations, you make it confusing and can feel like you have so much to move through.

How would being present benefit you in a current challenge situation?

How can you be present when you're over thinking about things?

Elly has also recommended me to read *The Power of Now* book by Eckhart Tolle. This book took me on a journey of self-realisation and allowed me to become aware of how I was responding to situations in my life. It taught me how to be present in everything I do. And when I started becoming present in my relationship at the time, I started to realise that this relationship wasn't doing me any good. I tried to be transparent and work through situations with him, but when push came to shove and nothing was progressing, I realised my **self-worth.**

OHHH ladies and gentlemen if you're reading this, self-worth is the most powerful trait any human being can develop for themselves. Once you mix acceptance with self-worth together, mmm you create a delicious recipe. Knowing what you deserve and accepting that another person cannot completely fulfill you, damn that's sexy and I am so proud of you for starting this journey.

A quote that really stood out to me in *The Power of Now* was *"The moment you realise you are not present, you are present. Whenever you are able to observe your mind, you are no longer trapped in it. Another factor has come in, something that is not of the mind: the witnessing presence."*

Your presence naturally shines a light on your self-worth and acceptance. I want to share with you my experience with not accepting my ex for who he was and how that affected me as a person. I must admit I struggled with this a lot because I *needed* my ex to be 'the way I wanted him to be'- why? Because my ego needed to be in control. We will talk about our ego shortly, but acceptance was a hard pill for me to swallow.

I needed my ex to show me affection, I needed him to put me first, I needed him to respond to me within a certain time frame, I needed him to be a certain way, and because of this we would always get into frequent arguments because he would never just be the way I wanted him to be.

I don't want you to get confused with understanding that there is a line between having your partner 'work with you' to ensure you both work together in a relationship compared to trying to make them become someone they're not.

The difference is, when you try to make your partner become and do something they aren't, it only creates chaos. Why? Well imagine you're in a relationship and your partner gets annoyed at you because you don't respond in the certain time frame that they want you to even though you were busy and they know that it is stressful for you to try to text while working or driving, or they don't show you affection in the same way you do. How would that make you feel? If you're single, still think about how that would make you feel if you had a partner wanting you to be a certain way that wasn't authentically you? I know I like the space of being able to make my own decisions without someone else on my back, so, why would your partner want you to be like that to them?

Working together in a relationship looks like both people understanding the middle line between their own, and their partners, wants and needs. We all have our own wants and needs that we would like our partner to work with, and I feel it's fair when both people work and agree in discussions together, rather than one person taking the reins and leading.

Not only that, when you accept your partner for who they are and have civil conversations about each other's differences, the relationship just flows differently.

Can you see the ripple effect of growing up without a stable father has had throughout my teenage and adult years?

Acceptance
/noun/

To believe what one is saying without questions or hesitation and to accept yourself without judgement.

I want you to take this moment and think back to your childhood and write down what comes up if you need (as writing is a good form of release). Think back to any happy and sad events in your childhood and reflect back on:

What happened?
Who was there?
And how did those events make you feel?

Then reflect on who you are as a person now, reflect on how you respond to situations when you are angry or annoyed at someone, or what other people do that triggers an emotional reaction from you. Through diving deep into your own experience, you slowly start to unpack the layers of who you are and realise the events that have occurred in your life and how it has influenced you while growing up.

This then links us into triggers.

What is your definition of a trigger?

For me it's feeling anxious and defensive because of something that's been said or done towards me. I know during my relationship with Josh I was triggered quite a lot because he wasn't as 'affectionate' as I wanted him to be. (This comes down to not having a male figure to show me the love and affection I wanted). He didn't 'post about me on his social media.' (I never felt wanted by a male in a relationship the way I felt I needed to be) He didn't go out of his way for me the way I would for him. (Which stems from never feeling like I mattered to a male) He never reassured me the way I wanted him too (I was scared he would leave, because I never had a stable male figure). In hindsight I could connect all the things I wanted from him to things I didn't receive as a child.

Everything I was doing slowly added up as to why I was reacting the way I did in my relationship with Josh. I could've easily put it all on him and said he never did this or that, *or* I could take responsibility by looking internally and ask myself *'why was I reacting and feeling that way?'*.

There were situations that happened throughout the relationship where he definitely could have handled things differently, but if he did, I probably wouldn't be here today writing this book about my journey. I'm a believer that everything happens for a reason, the good and the bad, and I believe I had to go through what I did in order to grow and become the person I am today. We are our own key to unlocking the door. This isn't a moment to place blame or guilt on ourselves, it's a moment to reflect, take self-responsibility, and take action to better ourselves. We don't always choose the situations we're dealt with in life; however, we can take action on how we respond to them. And our response is powerful.

I want you to know that we all have triggers. When you get angry, frustrated, and upset, think as to why are you feeling that way? What's triggering that emotion?

Avoiding your triggers isn't healing or productive. Avoiding your triggers is allowing your emotions to take control of you. Healing happens when you're triggered and you're able to move through the pain by feeling the emotion and bringing awareness to the trigger.

Triggers are teachers; thank them as they show you where healing is needed and redirect you to where you want to be.

E • go
/noun/

A person's sense of self-esteem or self-importance
"a boost to my ego"
The part of the mind that is between the conscious and the unconscious and is responsible for reality testing and a sense of personal identity.

Our ego's purpose is to protect us from the pain of the past and the future it predicts based on the past. Therefore, we'll find ourselves getting defensive and anxious when our partners don't show us enough affection, thinking they don't want us anymore or don't feel the same towards us because a previous partner has made us feel the same way. Our ego likes to repeat the same patterns of how we respond to situations when we feel a specific emotion because what the ego can predict, makes the ego feel safe. It will only allow you to see what fits its agenda as it is afraid of change.

Our Reticular Activating System (RAS) is located in the middle of our brain. Our RAS acts as a filter to all the "data" that is around us like; sounds, tastes, colours, and pictures. Any unnecessary noise or information that can interfere with the processing of messages don't make it through the filter for what we see and hear. It only lets in what it deems important. This is how sometimes we cannot see something that has been right in front of us, or how when you finally become aware of something you start to see it everywhere.

But how does it know what's important? It's what you focus on the most. Have you noticed people who say they aren't confident? Aren't confident. And those who say I'm always late, are ALWAYS late. Be very careful what you focus on, as it allows you to see that is who you are. So set your RAS to focus on the positives. I am confident, I am always on time, and watch as it begins to prove to you that your new beliefs are true by reflecting them in the world around you.

The ego keeps us addicted to the thoughts, feelings, and emotions we have experienced since childhood, because it is all way too familiar and that's exactly what it likes. It likes to protect our inner child because anything else that's 'new' to learn or do is too painful to acknowledge. As the ego's mind is insecure and has us feeling mentally distressed, causing us to feel uncomfortable by contrasting who we really are.

A great way to see and understand the difference between the ego state of mind, and the awareness state, is this graph below from Dr. Nicole LePera on The Holistic Psychologist.

Ego State	Awareness State
People's behaviour is personal	People's behaviours is a reflection of themselves.
Unconscious to patterns, habits, + behaviour	Aware of patterns, habits, + behaviour
Re-enacting my past experience in the present	Unlearning stories of my past to create a new future
People are good "good" or "evil"	People are unconscious
To receive love I must achieve, fulfil a role, or deny part of self.	I am worth of love just by fully expressing my highest self.

I want you to think about your ego. Where do you feel you are repeating and responding to situations the same way when the same emotions arise? How does your ego show up from your childhood experience?

Some tips to help overcome the way our ego runs our life:

- Let go of always needing to be in control.
- Let go of the need to always be right and win.
- Let go of needing to respond the same way when feeling the same emotions.
- Let go of the thought of not wanting to learn or acknowledge new information.
- Let go of comparing your relationships to others.
- Let go of getting into frequent arguments because of different points of views.
- Let go of wanting to fix and change other people.

Linking it all back to my childhood, if I had the role of a father while growing up, I believe I would've been able to handle situations differently, mainly my relationships with men. I believe I would've had the advice and support from a man's perspective. I have also seen through people close to me how having a supportive father, who has been there from the start, makes a difference on any child regardless of the gender. A good example of this is: I now see how my partner's dad is with his wife, (my partner's mum) I see how he speaks to his wife, treats her and the things he does for her. Then I look at my partner and how much he resembles his dad in the way he treats me. I can see how having his dad as a role model now reflects on my partner.

This is not to say if a person was to have their dad present it means they will be a good role model for them. It's when you do have a positive father figure in your life, the positive influences are quite noticeable. This is also not to say that men cannot be supportive and caring partners if they didn't grow up with a father figure, every individual will have a different experience in how their childhood affects them as adults. But it has been clear for me to see in others the link between growing up with supportive parents and the secure traits that brings out.

Key points:

Childhood triggers and traumas may look different in your situation but sit with some of the questions that were presented in the chapter and be honest and open with yourself. It may be daunting for some, but just remember you're uncovering the memories that have shaped you and you're providing yourself with the opportunity to move through each moment and heal from it.

Take a moment to think about your memories as a child?

- How do those memories make you feel?

- How have those memories shaped you?

- What situations or patterns seem to keep repeating in my life?

- What from your childhood could have influenced these behaviours and patterns?

I also would recommend discovering your love language. Discovering your love language will support you in finding your attachment style.

Head to: **www.5lovelanguages.com** whether you are single or in a relationship. Understanding your love language allows you to understand yourself better, because no one can understand you the way you understand yourself, right?

Note from me to you:
I want you to know whatever you may be dealing with from your childhood, it's okay to reach out for help. It's okay to ask close ones for advice, it's okay to speak up about how you're feeling, it's okay to seek professional help, and it's okay to seek new ways of self-healing. If anything, I highly recommend finding ways that work best for your healing journey.

You don't need to do it alone.

I didn't, and I couldn't have done it without those around me and the people that came into my life throughout my journey.

You've got this and I love you.

Two ♡
Hello Inner Child

Your inner child is your younger self that lives *within you*. You may remember her as the care-free two-year-old who loved to play, the anxious five-year-old who just wanted to be loved, or the reserved seven-year-old trying to fit in, or the sixteen-year-old who felt they needed to be in a relationship to feel loved. You have many energetic versions of your inner child within you through different ages, there will likely be one that is more prominent in your field.

Our inner child is the one that remembers the sweet gestures our grandma would do for us. It's the feeling of our heart brimming with love and joy when a family member would sing our favourite song or give us a hug, and it's also remembering being ignored and hurt from people we felt were meant to protect and love us unconditionally. Your inner child holds your innate innocence, curiosity, and also the pain of the first time you were hurt. How you cope as an adult is a reflection of the state you left your inner child during childhood and as you got older. As children we soak up and absorb how our parents, extended family, siblings, teachers, etc respond to us, this then becomes a reflection of how we respond to our external world.

The same person can have the same experiences in their childhood as you but interpret them differently and form different beliefs, therefore they are impacted differently in their adulthood. Our inner child is formed through the events that we experience *and* how we internalise them.

When you heal your inner child wounds and reconnect to who you are at your core, you will find a happy, bubbly, playful person within you, who is curious, bold, and wonderous. One who enjoys exploring, being open, and honest. Qualities we recognise in younger children that we somehow seem to leave behind in the process of growing up.

Our inner child is formed through different experiences, environments, and connections we encounter while growing up. As children we have certain needs for our development, some needs are universal, and some are specific to us. Some needs we may not have had met as children. Those needs could be - a connection with loved ones around us that felt safe, feeling a sense of belonging, receiving affection, attention, protection, guidance, and opportunities to be free and express ourselves. All of those needs are universal but the way they are met for different children can be varied and unique. In Chapter One we explored how not having a stable father figure had an effect on me which revealed itself when I started getting into relationships. In those situations, I subconsciously used the male figures to be my safe place. They made it feel 'normal' to me. As when I needed someone to talk to, they were there. When I felt lonely, they were there to hang out with. They were there most of the time when I needed them.

Our inner child will gravitate to what feels most comfortable and safe as it just wants to be loved and nurtured, as it's our younger self that didn't receive the love and nurture it wanted as a child. What feels 'normal' to our inner child may not actually be the most safe or loving environment for us now.

Inner child
/in· ner child/ noun

A hidden part of a person's personality that can be playful, joyous, creative, spontaneous, and usually accompanied by anger, hurt, and fear from their childhood.

I like to think of my inner child as that little girl within me who just wants to be happy and loved. But that little girl didn't receive the love she deserved and craved. So, now I get to treat her with love and she reminds me to be more loving and kinder to myself.

As a child I remember enjoying the moments of hanging out with my neighbours on a summer's day, eating multiple Zooper Doopers out the front of my lawn whilst feeling it melt away in my hands. I remember that my sister Tamara, younger brother Aron, and I would jump our back fence behind the paddock where we lived and we would run around making it back to our front yard before my dad had noticed we weren't there. It's memories like these that light up my inner child. That makes me feel happy, mischievous, playful, joyful, excited, grateful, and adventurous. And as I've grown up it's been important for me to remember to continue making space for my inner child through reading, going for walks, being outdoors, spending time with family, and painting.

What childhood memories can you remember and how did they make you feel now?

It's important for us as adults to look after and make space for our inner child, some of the ways you can do this are by:

- Meditating
- Journaling
- Taking a bath
- Listening to music and dancing
- Playing a board game
- Camping
- Playing with Lego or your favourite childhood toy
- Going to karaoke or singing in the shower
- Jumping on a trampoline
- Going to a playground
- Getting a massage
- Climbing trees
- Having a solo picnic
- Going to a concert
- Heading down to the beach and collecting shells

Creating a safe space for your inner child allows you to create a connection between what you do and how it makes you feel. Making time for your inner child allows you to unleash those feelings and emotions you used to feel as a child. It also allows you to be free and embrace what the moment has to offer.

Becoming conscious of how I'm feeling has allowed me to be aware of when I've been neglecting my inner child. If reading this has made you feel as though you have been neglecting your inner child, I get you, I feel you, I've been there too. Our lives can get busy with so many distractions and responsibilities, use this book will guide you to reconnect with your inner child.

I like to put my headphones on while I am on the train heading into work to utilise that as my down time. This makes me feel relaxed and content as I'm not rushing to do anything, I'm just enjoying the moment.

When you realise you've been neglecting your needs, your self-worth, or you sacrifice too much for others, get a photo of you as a child. Look at her and ask yourself, would you treat the girl in that photo the way you treat yourself now?

We can spend so much time giving our energy to other people and doing certain things that we seem to forget about ourselves. Are we not aware of the importance of looking after ourselves? Or do we not know how too? And this is why I'm here, I'm here to remind you that your inner child wants you to give them attention, wants you to give them love, wants you to recognise them. Show that baby girl you still love her and that you're here for her.

As there is duality to every experience we encounter, there is also duality to our inner child. Understanding duality is knowing that in any given situation two opposing ideas and feelings can exist at the same time. When it comes to our inner child we can always experience hurt and neglect *as well* as joy and happiness simultaneously. Becoming comfortable with accepting both of these experiences allows you to know that you can be happy even when parts of your inner child are hurting, and you can be hurting even when your inner child is happy.

Self-love
/self-luv/ noun

To love and appreciate oneself. To take care of one's needs and well-being without sacrificing to please others. To know that you are worthy of respect and kindness from others, but most importantly yourself. Nourish and flourish your body, mind, and soul.

Breaking the cycle of how we've been treating ourselves or what we do for ourselves allows us to break through the cycle of feeling and having stagnant energy within our bodies. As what we repeat, we don't repair.

It's time to drop those misconceptions about our childhood trauma. People tend to think of trauma as abuse, however, that's not all what trauma is. Trauma is an unreleased emotional response to an event often having long-lasting mental-effects OR any physical damage to the body caused by emotional distress. Over time this imbalance manifests as 'problems' throughout our life as it's the body's and mind's wiring that brings us back into balance and allows us to self-regulate.

Have you ever been told "oh don't worry about that, it's all in the past?" What's happened throughout our past, our childhood, will always come back and re-visit us throughout our adult life and relationships. As explored in Chapter One, the first five years of a child's life is crucial as that's when the brain is most immature and develops based on a child's environment and interactions.

I would recommend seeking professional support during times of bringing up and releasing childhood trauma. Sometimes when doing the inner work of our inner child we may suppress memories of abuse or intense situations and find they may arise during this time. Seek professional to support and guide you through the journey if needed, they will support you through the healing process.

What do you think of when you hear the phrase 'inner child'?

When I first heard it, I had no idea what it meant. I remember hearing those around me speaking about it and was intrigued, so I looked it up on the internet to only still have no idea what it meant. I then started meditating and journaling and through my own experiences, I was then able to slowly pull it all together. As easy as it is for me to say you can do x,y,z it's not until you put the words to actions that you will begin to notice how connecting with your inner child makes you feel.

Heal • ing
/noun/

The process of becoming or making somebody healthy again; the process of getting better after emotional distress. It's the process of restoring your health.

Let's try and get to notice when your inner child becomes triggered, so you can become aware of where your actions are stemming from. You might notice there is a pattern to how you respond to situations, for example, during relationships when your partner doesn't give you the 'amount' of affection you want or when someone speaks to you in a certain way. A trigger is anything that generates an emotionally charged response.

Tapping into my inner child has allowed me to forgive myself for how I treated myself during past relationships, all the sacrifices I've made, all the harsh words and thoughts I used to say to myself, and all the people who I've allowed to hurt me. In order to move through events that have happened to us in our life we need to tap into them. To tap into an event, is to dive deeper into a situation and discover why we are treating ourselves the way we do? What do we achieve when we respond like that?

The first step to healing your inner child is to acknowledge that you need to heal your *childhood trauma*. In Chapter One, we go through examples of what I've experienced while growing up and have seen how evident it was throughout my life when growing up. Tapping into it allows you to understand yourself better, allows you to become more comfortable within yourself, and teaches you how to love yourself through the moments of distress, it's forgiving how you once treated your inner child, and yourself now.

Healing our inner child helps us heal by tapping into our vulnerable self.

What repeated patterns have you been doing and still are that's making your inner child feel 'safe,' and as you've grown up you realise that this isn't how you want to treat yourself anymore?

I want you to honour that little girl inside of you, that little girl was hurt, abused, and abandoned and felt like she wasn't enough. It's now time to let her truly feel safe, let her know that she is loved, tell her every day how special she is, she deserves it. Keep her clean, warm, and nourish her with nutritious foods. Let her be free, let her embrace doing everything she loves, riding her bike, doing cartwheels, eating ice cream, or rolling her roller blades, painting, running, and swimming. It might sound silly, but honouring that little girl inside of you is going to bring you so much joy and fulfilment. That little version of you still exists so give her the love and care that she needs, that she didn't receive as a child.

She is powerful.

Key points:

Affirmations to heal your inner child:
- I am enough, I have always been enough, and I will always continue to be enough. Nothing external can change that.
- My parents' mistakes are a reflection of their journey, not mine.
- I love you, I hear you, I see you.
- I honor you, I appreciate you, I admire you.

Questions to heal your inner child: *Trust whatever comes up when answering*
- What and who hurt my inner child?
- What pattern have I developed and repeated from my experience of pain?
- What needs were not met while growing up?
- What makes me feel most at peace?
- Where and who can I focus my forgiveness on?

As there is duality to your inner child, asking yourself questions like these will allow you to feel different emotions:
- What was your favourite childhood memory?
- Why was it your favourite memory?
- How were you feeling during that moment?

- Write a letter to your inner child. Describe how you felt during certain situations at different points of your life.

And most importantly:

Acknowledge what has happened
Accept what you can't control
Address what you *can* control

"The power for creating a better future is contained in the present moment: You create a good future by creating a good present."- Eckhart Tolle

Three ♡

Discovering who you are

By now I feel you are wanting to dive deeper to discover more of who you are and how your experiences throughout your life have contributed to your personality, traits, and beliefs. You may also be asking yourself 'how does my mind influence events that have occurred throughout my life?' My goal is that by the end of this chapter you understand the role your mindset plays in who you are.

Before we get into discovering how and why our experiences have shaped who we are, I want you to think about where it all began? Where the traits of kindness, love, and generosity came from, or where the greedy, disrespectful, and biased traits come from? There's only one thing that comes into my mind after re-visiting Chapter One and Two, that it's our environment we've been around throughout our childhood and adolescent stage.

Our brain is known to reflect everything we know in our environment. All the experiences and events we have been through have been stored in the brain's synaptic connections. A synapse is an area where two neutrons come close enough to one another that they are able to pass chemical signals from one cell to another. As Dr. Joe Dispenza says in his book *Breaking the Habit of Being Yourself,* "the relationships with people we've known, the variety of things we own and are familiar with, the places where we've visited and lived at different times in our lives, and the experiences myriad embraced throughout our years are all configured in the structures of the brain."

I want you to give yourself time to answer these questions and see what comes up.

- What kind of person have I been?
- What type of person do I think I am?
- What type of person have I presented to the world?
- How would my family and friends describe me?

While answering these questions explore what comes up and just know that whatever comes up is exactly what's meant to come up. Whether the thoughts of feeling like you have sacrificed too much of yourself for others or you think you've been seen as a people pleaser. I'd like to invite you to dig deeper as to why you have sacrificed yourself for others or why you felt you've been a people pleaser?

When I was presented with these questions, it came to surface that I was sacrificing too much of myself for other people, and so I explored how that made me feel. It made me feel exhausted, drained, and sad. I felt heavy always trying to do my best to help people even on a half empty cup. I would pour so much of myself into other people and would forget about the most important person… me.

From sitting with answers that came up I decided to evolve from them. I realised I didn't want to feel like that anymore and worked on saying to people "I'd love to help you, but I'm sorry I can't" and the more I said it, the more I realised the person I have been and the person I am now.

Allowing yourself to ask and sit with the answers to these questions allows you to dive deeper into who you are, understand why you have been feeling the way you do, but also allows you to be aware of the person you were and the person you want to be.

Creating your own happiness:

What is your life purpose?

I know my life purpose is to be happy and being happy can look different for many of us. I realised happiness was my life purpose, as I would have moments of driving in my car and feeling the sun beaming down on me. I had my music on and just felt so happy with where I was at in my life and everything that's happening in that moment. I was able to acknowledge the positives and how good I felt while also being able to acknowledge that I'm not always going to feel like this, however, I know I can move through any other feeling that arises by meditating or doing breathwork. I know that I'm in control of how I feel and I can choose what I would like to do.

For some people their purpose may be connected to something that satisfies them, for example: doing an activity that contributes to their pleasure. Others may find their purpose in their responsibilities they have with their family or friends, and some may seek their life purpose through their spirituality or cultural beliefs. Our lives are constantly changing, and some may feel their life purpose can evolve as they level up to be the best version of them, and some may be fixated on the one purpose that brings them happiness. Explore your life purpose, get to know yourself better and you'll be able to understand what your life purpose is.

Conscious and Subconscious Mind:

The conscious mind can be described as alive, awake, aware, anything you are currently aware of. It's actively processing what you're feeling, seeing, touching, doing, or experiencing. Our conscious mind can only hold one thought at a time as it analyses, thinks, plans, and has short term memory. For example: If you go to cross the road and hear a car coming, you instantly look into the direction of where the car is coming.

Our subconscious mind is a large memory bank that stores unlimited memories, beliefs, or fears that we've experienced over time. The role of our subconscious mind is to store and retrieve data that helps us to respond in the way we've been programmed. So we don't need to give conscious thought to how we will walk or reach for something, we just do it. Some programming is very helpful to our lives and some is not. It allows us to feel and remember our emotions, habits, relationship patterns, intuition, and has long term memory. The subconscious mind controls 95% of our thoughts, actions, and behaviours which ultimately shapes a lot of our life. As Dr. Joe Dispenza says "about 95% of who we are by midlife is a series of subconscious programs that have become automatic" Our subconscious programming often takes us into autopilot where we're absent minded and simply act without thought. For example: If you feel nervous, you may start biting your nails instinctually without any thought or awareness. This is where you may catch yourself doing something and then when you begin to think consciously again you may regret it or realise just how absent minded you were in that moment. You may even forget why you even started doing a particular thing, like when you open the pantry out of habit but you aren't sure if you actually needed anything out of it.

It's always actively working in the background and most of the time we are not aware of it. Because of this, it influences how we respond to situations, for example: Why we sometimes binge a whole packet of chips without realising until we get to the last one, or why we blurt what we were thinking before giving consideration as to how others may feel, or why we can drive all the way home with no conscious thought of where we're turning. On the flip side, the subconscious mind also contributes to things like; why you're motivated, confident, and successful. The subconscious mind doesn't think, it remembers. It's driven based on our programming and reinforces habits. Some of those habits support us, for example: When nourishing our body and moving in a way that supports our strength and mobility. Learning how to program the subconscious mind to support the vision you have for your life and the person you want to be is a powerful thing for your life. As the programmed subconscious mind leads us to 95% of our actions, thoughts and behaviours.

Vietnamese Zen Master Thuong Chieu once said, "when we understand how our mind works, our practice becomes easy." To understand our minds, we need to understand our consciousness.

When we understand our minds, we are able to have more control over how to use the combined power of our conscious and subconscious minds to think in a more healthy, resilient, and flexible way. Understanding our consciousness is having the awareness of each individual thought and feelings that arise.

When we learn to understand our minds, we learn to reprogram it and we learn to see the positives in any given situation without self-sabotaging. Let yourself grow, let yourself heal. We are our own healers and healing is the journey back to our authentic self.

The methods I have found that work best to reprogram the subconscious mind is through repetition and heightened emotions. Throughout my journey with my mind, I know it would distract me when I would lay down during meditation. As soon as I would lay down, I would feel the need to open my eyes and when I would open my eyes, I would think to myself "oh okay, why did you open them, close your eyes again." It was with repetition of consciously reminding myself that I am safe where I am and knowing the benefits of the meditations without being distracted, I continuously kept doing them until I had control over my mind and would lay down during meditations that went for ten minutes. I felt so good after it. I needed the repetition of meditating lying down for my subconscious to alter the programming of feeling uncomfortable and distracted while laying down.

We see this style of repetition used in the programming of children often, when a child learns to walk and falls down for the first time, no one expects them to not try to walk or stand up again. We continuously provide positive encouragement and support the child to get back up again and keep trying. The repetition is combined with the heightened emotions of encouragement. However, with adults, we can try something for the first time and think we can never do it and don't give ourselves any encouragement or enough time to do it again.

We need to start respecting and understanding ourselves, knowing that it's okay if you don't 'get it done' or 'complete it' the first time you try. It's time to start being gentler and more compassionate to your inner child. I understand it can be challenging if you grew up where you were criticised for trying new things and weren't given the opportunity to try it again. From this experience it can become embedded into us and this is how we are conditioned to think that we aren't good at doing anything. Our subconscious mind has stored memories from what has happened to us including our childhood memories. The truth is, it takes awareness and getting uncomfortable to get out of our minds and start taking action for ourselves.

Another method I have found that has worked is through heightened emotions. I spoke about positive affirmations in Chapter Two and as amazing as they are to say, I believe there is a difference between saying words and believing them too. To believe the words you need to have a level of emotion in them to understand the words you say, and how they make you feel. For example: Instead of saying the positive affirmation 1,000 times to reprogram through repetition, we can repeat it just 100 times and bring heightened emotions into it to get the same result. Throughout my journey I've experienced heightened emotions during the process of forgiving my ex. As I was journaling, I wrote about the relationship as I knew writing it down was a way for me to release it from my body and that it would allow me to forgive him and move forward from it. While doing so, heightened emotions arose and I remember sitting on my bed starting to feel sensitive and heavy. I felt my eyes start to water and fill up and as they got full the emotional release made me feel so much lighter. I felt like I unlocked the gate into the enchanted forest. I felt free from those feelings and felt like it was no longer in my thoughts. At that point I knew I was able to finally move forward from it.

As you travel through this book, I want you to know that these are my experiences, you may experience something similar or you may experience something different. Take the lessons and apply them into your own life.

Understanding our brain:

Dr. Joe Dispenza is a master that talks about evolving our brain and the science behind changing our minds. I could listen to him talk on YouTube and read his book over and over again, he is so knowledgeable and I have learnt so much from just reading his *Breaking the Habit of Being Yourself.* In this book, Dr. Joe Dispenza talks about overcoming our body and our mind and that every time we have a thought there is a biochemical reaction created in our brain. Your brain then realises over time to release a specific chemical signal to our body where they act as messengers of thought. Dr. Joe Dispenza shares that "when the body gets these chemical messages from the brain, it complies instantly by initiating a matching set of reactions directly in alignment with what the brain is thinking. Then the body immediately sends a confirming message back up to the brain that it's now feeling exactly the way the brain is thinking."

Neurotransmitters, neuropeptides, and hormones are the cause-and-effect chemicals for brain activity and bodily functioning. Dr. Joe Dispenza sums them up by saying "think of neurotransmitters as chemical messengers primarily from the brain and mind, neuropeptides as chemical signalers that serve as a bridge between the brain and the body to make us feel the way we think, and hormones as the chemicals related to feelings primarily in the body." And an example he provides of this is when you have a sexual fantasy all three of these factors are at work in action together. Dr. Joe Dispenza says "First as you start to think a few thoughts, your brain whips up some neurotransmitters that turn on a network of neurons, which creates pictures in your mind. These chemicals then stimulate the release of specific neuropeptides into your bloodstream. Once they reach your sexual glands, those peptides bind to the cells of those tissues; they turn on your hormonal system, and-presto- things start happening." From this you have created a fantasy with your thoughts that feels so real in your body, that your body starts preparing for an actual sexual experience (ahead of the event). That's how powerful your mind and body are.

Mind blowing right? So now we have an understanding of how powerful our mind is to create an experience from a thought that affects our body. I want you to take a moment to think about what other experiences you can create in relation to discovering who you are? Think about the power of your thoughts and how you can tweak the words you say in your mind or how you speak about yourself, or something you're experiencing, in order to change how you feel.

Now is the time:

It's now time to commit and work through discovering who you are.

The first step is to get uncomfortable. Be uncomfortable with stepping out of your subconscious mind and unravel who you are when you respond to situations and the conditions you've adapted to when growing up. Once you're aware of it, it's then accepting that's what you grew up with, and think about the type of person you want to be. This is where growth stems from.

I choose to live my life now reflecting on the ways I could be holding myself back that I may regret in 50 years. When I was initially confronted with this idea, it really hit home for me thinking of the way I was programmed to act as a young girl and how that was still influencing me. While growing up I was quite a shy girl. I wouldn't say boo to anyone, if my sister and I went out with friends she would be the one doing all the talking and I would only speak if spoken to. And every day I constantly had that thought of 'what would I regret not doing in 50 years' time' stuck in my head on repeat, because I truly didn't want to be that quiet girl who was 'shy and thought she didn't have the confidence within' anymore. I didn't want to look back when I was older and regret the things I could've done knowing we only live once.

So, one day I made the decision within myself that I was going to do the things I had always wanted to do. I wanted to start enjoying life, I wanted to be happy, I wanted to be free, I wanted to be confident, and I didn't want to hold back on things that deep down I knew I wanted to do. Knowing that I wanted to gain more confidence within me, I also knew I had to break out of my comfort zone and if I'm being honest with you, it wasn't easy but it was definitely worth it. One thing I have learnt on my journey of growth is to enjoy the process. Sometimes we get so caught up in the end result, we forget the most important part, the process, as that's where we learn and grow the most, that's where we step out of our comfort zone.

Every time I went to start a conversation when I was in a group of people, I would get quite nervous and my mind would tell me 'I couldn't do it.' This would happen two, three, even four times. Though, with knowing the power of positive affirmations, I would constantly tell myself each time 'no I can do it, and I will.' I remember each time I told myself that I would hold a conversation a little longer than I did previously and I remember the moment so clearly when I held a conversation with someone I just met, feeling on top of the world. I was so happy like a kid that's just won a toy out of a claw machine. I remember feeling the excitement of accomplishment as I did it and I knew I could. I'll never forget the first moment.

Once you learn to step out of your comfort zone you not only feel a whole lot better, but you see the world from a different perspective. You're able to take that step back and think about the choices, decisions, and opportunities you want to engage in. You're able to make those choices based on how you're feeling with knowing and understanding how you may feel after it.

Once you've dived deeper into discovering who you are, it's then time to hold yourself accountable for how you speak, act, and relate to others. We will explore more about your relationship with others in Chapter Four. This will allow you to get clearer on who you are, as how you speak and act to others, allows your subconscious mind to determine who you are.

Just for a moment, I want you to stop and think about what it means to be "conscious?"

Hey, what are you doing reading this sentence? I just asked you a question, have you actually thought about it?

I promise you, answering it will change your perspective on how you approach situations.

I also mentioned in Chapter One: *The Power of Now* book by Eckhart Tolle. I truly can't recommend this book enough to anyone who wants to learn about 'how to be present in each moment.' This book allowed me to see how I was responding to situations on a conscious level, where I was able to have a thought and acknowledge that thought from a distance without having any feelings or attachments to the thought. It allowed me to look internally before externally as I used to try and search for everything I was missing in other people, such as; the confidence to step out of my comfort zone and the ability to love myself. And from reading this book I learnt to take my power back and build the confidence and self-love I already had in me and learnt to embrace it with everything I got.

Learning to look internally and not externally in every situation has allowed me to discover who I was and grow as an individual. As when I discovered my triggers and how I contributed to a situation, I was then able to learn and choose how I wanted to respond to situations.

I mentioned in Chapter One about how I discovered the Bloom app and the benefits of discovering meditation. I want you to find and discover what works for you. I remember paying for a two-week subscription because I wasn't sure I'd like the app only to then pay for a yearly one after it expired. I remember listening to the guided meditation for the first-time while fidgeting, constantly opening my eyes before I could sink into it and enjoy it. However, I kept persisting. I set a goal for myself, which I now call having a 'non-negotiable', that I would meditate at least two times a week. There were times after purchasing the yearly subscription that I didn't mediate for a whole week. Though, I would acknowledge it, and would ensure I got myself back into it, as I knew how it made me feel.

We've all heard that saying 'consistency is the key'. To stay consistent is to be consistent with those healthy routines that we do daily that enable us to live a healthier and happier life. The repetition of these routines helps us reprogram our subconscious mind, which then supports us to form habits that we effortlessly continue. The habits are reinforced by the belief that we program into our subconscious- that we can do it.

Intuition:

Connecting to your intuition will empower to empower you when you begin to understand it. By listening to your intuition, you are guiding yourself as you build trust with yourself to understand a feeling instinctively. Intuition is said to be the spiritual connection to our subconscious as that's how our subconscious and conscious minds communicate. Albert Einstein once said "the intuitive mind is a sacred gift and the rational mind is a faithful servant."

Have you ever felt that nudge in your gut when you're in a sticky situation and your mind isn't sure what to do but you have this feeling in your stomach that is telling you to do the opposite thing to what logic would suggest? That my friend is your gut feeling and I know you've heard of it before, but are you in tune with it? Do you follow its guidance for you or do you go against it? If you do follow it, how does it make you feel? If you don't follow it, how does that make you feel?

Tuning into intuitive messages from your body can take some time and practice. When we have that consistent relationship with our body, we're able to respond to what our intuition is telling us. I connect to my intuition through two different ways, the first one is by asking myself questions and allowing my body to respond by what comes up, whether it's in a thought or feeling and the second way is when a thought appears about my career, relationship, or a situation I'm in and I tune deeper into it by asking myself, "what is it that I need reminding of, or what do I need to learn from this?"

Those who are clairvoyant would connect into their intuition in more of a visual way, by seeing images usually in their mind. Those who are clairsentience are able to identify intuitive messages through their feelings, and those who are claircognizance have a clear knowing through the mind. There are other clair-abilities with our intuition being able to speak to us through different senses and sensations of the body. With practice and tuning into your body, you'll be able to find and connect with your own version of intuition. This may look like one of these above or it could be a combination of them but with practice you'll be able to understand how your intuition feels and speaks in your body.

Being true to yourself:

Do you ever do things that don't sit right with you, or you feel you're doing them because your friends are doing it? Yeah, me too. I've been there and experienced it and can tell you the only way to acknowledge if you're doing what doesn't align with the person you know you are, is to ask yourself; 'am I being true to myself? Am I doing everything that aligns with the person I am? Is this the type of person I am?'. Is it coming from a place of not feeling good enough, limited beliefs or fears of disappointment and judgement? Sit with it and see what comes up.

I also want to touch on the fact that way others speak to you is a reflection of how they speak to themselves. Don't ever feel or believe you deserve to be spoken to in a certain way. Sometimes it happens instantly and out of nowhere and sometimes you know how a person communicates. Just know the way anyone speaks to you is a reflection of them, it's a reflection of the relationship they have with themselves and everything around them, it's the way they view their world. At times this may be hard to understand as we have emotions and feel things, though once you learn to accept how people are, you won't ever question who you are as a person.

The most beautiful thing about life is that you can always change, evolve, and become more of who you truly are. You aren't defined by your past and mistakes. On the popular *To Be Magnetic* (@tobemagnetic) Instagram page where they share neuroscience and psychology information, they made a post that I fully agree with saying - "when we fully embody who we are, we stop looking for the lost parts of ourselves in other people."

I want to seal this chapter with this; while discovering who you are, you need to be committed to wanting to create a change, you need to be open and willing to step outside of your comfort zone. You need to understand and remember that when you have great or loving thoughts you produce those chemicals in your brain and you then begin to feel that way, and same goes for negative and anxious thoughts, your body will start to feel that way in seconds. And that is how powerful our thoughts and minds are.

It's not a short-term quick fix, but you'll reap the long-term benefits.

Key points:

- *"Warning:* when feelings become the means of thinking, or if we cannot think greater than how we feel, we can never change. To change is to think greater than how we feel"- Dr. Joe Dispenza
- Reading 'Breaking the Habit of Being Yourself' will allow you to understand how your mind works and how it shapes your life, this understanding can change your life and allow you to create a new one.
- Asking yourself these questions can allow you to understand yourself better:

    o What kind of person have I been?
    o What type of person do I think I am?
    o What type of person have I presented to the world?

- Now is the time to think about the life you want to live and how are you going to create it?

WHO ARE YOU?

Beyond your fears. Beyond your subconscious programming. Beyond the expectations of others. Beyond what you experienced during your childhood. Beyond your mistake you've made and the judgements you've placed on yourself?

Dream big my friends, you've picked up this book and started reading it because something about the title, blurb, or even reading the first few pages have attracted you to it. This means you've already made a conscious decision to yourself that you know you want to do better for yourself. Don't let how you have been conditioned to think and feel control how you live your life.

You   are   in   control.

"*Fall in love with taking care of yourself.* Fall in love with the path of deep healing. Fall in love with becoming the best version of yourself but with *patience*, with compassion and respect to your own journey."- Sylvester McNutt

Four ♡

Who are you in your relationship?

The journey of who you are in your relationships has a significant impact on who you are as a person. I'm not just talking about intimate relationships, I'm talking about relationships with your parents, siblings, and friends, even acquaintances and the one-sided relationships you can have with people like celebrities. Each relationship has varying degrees of influence and relevance in your life.

Who are you within each of your relationships?

Do you know yourself inside and out? Do you know your strengths, weaknesses, your behaviour, tendencies, and thought pattern?

To know who you are in your relationships you have to be super clear on who you are in the absence of your relationships.

When we don't know who we are as a person and who we are in our relationships, we sometimes make choices that don't always sit well with us. For example; because I didn't know who I was in my relationship with my ex and I was seeking external validation, I would only go to the gym because he did, as I needed to look and feel good just like him. But if I loved, and was clear, on who I was, I would've made a clear decision and knew what I wanted to do.

What sparks that joy inside of you? What gives you strength? What drains you? In Chapter Three we talked about discovering who you are with many prompts to help you in your own exploration.

My intention behind asking these questions is because in any interaction you have it's so important that you enter it as a whole person with a clear set of energetic boundaries. I want you to stop thinking about allowing another person to complete you, which we also spoke about in Chapter One when I shared my story of using my ex to be the creator of my happiness.

Being grounded in who you are and having a conscious awareness of that, means that when you are with others you don't get completely uprooted and completely change who you are to mould yourself into something you think the other person will like or accept. Without a clear grounding it is easier to lose connection with who you really are and this makes you more susceptible to boundaries being crossed before you have the space to realise it.

The Law of Rhythm + The Law of Vibration = happy oneself.

The Law of Rhythm is a two and from measured movement, with an inflow and outflow, a swing backward and forward, waves going in and out. Everything follows a process in a rhythmic pattern.

It's really easy to believe that you are amazing, life loves you, you're amazing at your job, your relationship and family life are going amazing, when life is going well for you. Though, what if something appears to not go your way for a moment, are you willing to still believe that you are amazing, competent, and capable at what you do and in who you are? Or are you going to change your beliefs and turn in against yourself?

Is the person you are when everything is going well, different when something doesn't go your way?

The Law of Rhythm in action looks like- Jane who is a retail worker, works at the second highest ranked organic food company in the world. Jane has just broke her highest record in sales for a single month. She happy in her relationship and her family life is going great. Jane knows she's amazing at her job, she has great relationships with her colleagues and customers. However, Jane starts to become frustrated as she finds out that her biggest customers have started shopping elsewhere and she starts to turn her frustration into fear as she feels her sales will drop. If Jane wasn't grounded in who she is, she could internalise this and make it mean something about herself, that she isn't as amazing, capable, and competent as what she thought she was, she doesn't have a great relationship with customers like she thought she did, she would start to spiral and try to connect her customers shopping elsewhere with something being inherently wrong with her, she would likely have a mini-identity crisis. This then may bleed into her relationships within her personal life, and her relationship with herself. By not being grounded within herself, this could trigger Jane to feel rejected, abandoned, and jealous that her customers have gone elsewhere. A small event spirals into stories that will likely lead her into self-criticism and unnecessary changes. What would happen if Jane was grounded within herself?

If Jane was grounded within herself and had a strong concept of who she is, she wouldn't blink an eye and wouldn't begin to question how she thinks of herself, as she knows who she is and what she's capable of achieving. Jane may feel frustrated for a moment but ultimately, she would be happy for her customers as they have found someone else and this is making space for new customers and new opportunities to enter her space, and she doesn't need customers to believe that she is good at her job for her to believe in herself. She may reflect on improving skills related to her work but as she is grounded in who she is as a person, she doesn't link any of this reflection back to her innate qualities.

Understanding the Law of Rhythm allows us to accept all phases of life with a new perspective that allows us to be understanding and compassionate to ourselves while experiencing the ups and downs of life - as it's inevitable.

Understanding the Law of Rhythm in relationships allows us to understand that you can give to others, however, there is the cause and effect when you realise the other person isn't giving back. This is why it's so important to understand who you are in relationships and important to have energetic boundaries, as it prevents you from to taking on the emotional feelings of others. It allows us to be clear in who we are, our thoughts and feelings, and allows us to respond effectively. When I was in a relationship with my ex, I felt like I had no concept of who I was and what my energetic boundaries were. Because of this, I found myself sacrificing my needs for his. I kept pouring from an empty cup and I found myself not knowing when to say 'that's okay, you're like that, I'm going to do this instead' and I continued doing everything to suit him. This meant that when my ex and I would have a disagreement, I would continue to keep pursuing the disagreement in order to get the response I thought I needed at the time, but I didn't and we never came out of our disagreements happy or with a clear resolution that benefited us both. However, if I followed through with the Law of Rhythm and accepted that was his response to me, the outcome would've been different. As time went on and in Chapter One, I spoke about where I discovered meditation, and how it taught me to accept things I couldn't control, and when I did the universe would redirect me in another direction. In a positive direction, in a direction of realisation, of awareness of the relationship I was in, how it was making me feel and what I wanted for myself.

The Law of Vibration is where everything has a unique vibrational frequency. Everything in the universe vibrates in its own frequency and things with a similar frequency are drawn together. Our feelings and thoughts are what essentially impact our vibrational frequency, as Abraham Hicks says "as you think, you vibrate. As you vibrate, you attract." When you're vibrating at a higher level, you'll feel lighter and more at ease and when vibrating at a lower frequency it feels heavy and dark. When you vibrate at a higher frequency you experience, and have, greater personal power, you're able to think with more clarity, you know what you want, you feel at peace with yourself and your surroundings, you enjoy life with love and joy. When you're vibrating at a lower frequency it's hard to get out of your own mind, you may feel sad and stressed.

When you have negative feelings and thoughts about yourself within a relationship, any type of relationships, you will be vibrating at a lower frequency and as the Law of Vibration works closely with manifesting, when you manifest the type of relationships you want, you allow yourself to have those type of relationships. Manifesting is a practice that brings awareness to everything you say. For example, you might say, "I wish I was rich." If you continue to say 'you wish' that's what you're sending out to the universe which is what you're manifesting, but if you changed your wording to 'I am rich', you're putting out a higher frequency message and you're bringing that positive energy in as you're saying and going on with your life in the energy of a rich person. As I explored in the last chapter, it is not the affirmation or words on their own that hold power, it is the words along with our energy and emotions that shift our frequency.

You can raise your vibration in many ways that incorporate your daily routine, you may not realise that there are many things you are already doing that are raising your vibration. Anything you enjoy doing supports you in raising your vibration as it makes you happy (a higher frequency emotion). Below are some examples for ways you can raise your vibration; these examples support boosting your mind and mood which then affects how you are throughout your day.

Some examples you may like that raise your vibration are by:
- Writing down what you're grateful for at home, work or even people.

- Meditate daily.
- Going to an art class, where you release your creativity through different materials.
- Eating healthy foods that give you energy and nourish your body.
- Doing yoga, where you stretch and move your energy throughout your body.
- Enjoy spending time in nature getting some sun, some vitamin D.
- Dancing, giving yourself opportunities to allow your energy to flow through and around you.

Ways to lower your vibration:
- Thinking negative constantly sets your mindset to that level and brings those negative feelings.
- Eating excessive junk food that makes your stomach feel ill, and you begin to feel sluggish, fatigued, and start craving more sugar.
- Staying indoors for an excessive amount of time where you don't see natural light, as seeing at least 10 minutes of natural light per day is conducive with higher vibrational health.
- Watching too much TV where you feel sluggish and fatigue and don't really do much with your day. Your eyes begin to hurt and your body isn't moving.

- Feeling angry without allowing it in a healthy expression.
- Being lazy and not productive with your day.

There are 10 other laws of the universe that could play a big part in your journey, explore them if that feels fun for you.

It's time to start thinking about who YOU are in your relationships and how your relationships impact you. Being in the relationship with my ex made me extra sensitive and emotional and made me feel as though it was hard to trust others again. Sometimes we feel that just because we *only* have one relationship where we feel unhappy, that it doesn't affect us in our other relationships. And I'm referring to all relationships, and this is why I want you to ask yourself these questions and see what comes up.

Do you know how you are in your relationships?
How do your relationships impact you?
How do different perceptions impact you?

We have relationships with everything we encounter or engage with. For example: If you're reading a long novel that you're really enjoying, you build a relationship with it and grow an attachment to picking it up every day and reading it. If you had a favourite water bottle and then lost it, you had grown to like it and were used to having it every day, so now that it's no longer around you feel sad and lost without it. If you met a new friend and have built a good relationship with them. We build relationships with everything within our environment and it's important to understand who you are in those relationships.

Relationships within our immediate family have an immense influence on our relationships with ourselves, if you grew up with your parents making you feel worthless by saying "you're useless, you do nothing," you're going to grow up and see yourself as 'useless' as a person but also in your relationships, sometimes this can be at a deeper subconscious level that you are not consciously aware of. And reflecting back you will be able to see how that affected you while growing up. Linking back to our inner child in Chapter Two. The influences of our environment, our upbringing, and how we become conditioned to think and feel a certain way based on experiences we have encountered.

If you're in a relationship with a man who is wounded in his masculine, you may feel the need to take on the masculine energy and may find yourself being the strong one in the relationship that takes control, and over time you'll feel the exhaustion from it. If you're in a relationship and you have wounded masculine energy, you may feel in your relationships that you struggle to feel safe, that you are wanting your partner to protect and love you, you're scared to fail, you may be cold and distant, you may defend yourself and verbally attack your partner as you can't be wrong. If you have wounded feminine energy you may find yourself looking for external validation in others, you're insecure, you go out seeking love in the wrong places, and you have low self-worth. Something I did!

Growing up with an absent dad and seeing myself go in and out of the relationships, it is very clear to me how wounded my masculine and feminine energy was. I always had to feel safe, protected, and loved so I would sacrifice my wants and my needs for my ex. I wasn't great with communication and when we had a disagreement, I would go cold and distant myself from him, to the point where I would need him to approach me first, and I would always defend myself during disagreements as I didn't have any self-worth.

What can you relate too? Which energy are you wounded in? Which part are you reading over and going 'a-huh that's me!'?

By looking outward at the many perceptions of you it is easy to completely lose a sense of who you are. Without a strong sense of who you are, you can move through life without a clear sense of what you want, what you stand for, how you want to live, and who you want to be. Your raw emotions and fears rule your life trying to seek approval in a way you never really can, because you can never be someone that all people in the world will love, and accept, all at once.

Rather, start pulling your energy inwards, to see who you are within yourself and to know what you stand for. So that you can actually be in relationships with others as your real self and so you can give others the opportunity to get to know the real you.

While you hide under a mask of what you think others might want you to be, your relationships will stay at the surface while no one will get the opportunity to love the real you.

Who are you in your relationships?
Are you yourself?

Key points:

- It's time to really start thinking about who you are in your relationships. Are the friends you're around supportive you; do they fill your cup up, do they encourage you to be the best you can be?
- Understanding how The Law of Rhythm and The Law of Vibration interwinds with you and your relationships is the first step that supports you with setting your energetic boundaries.

Manifesting Mantras to boost your vibration:

- I accept myself unconditionally
- All I need is within me
- I attract love, success, relationships, and freedom
- Opportunities will always come my way
- I am becoming the best version of myself
- My thoughts become my reality

Start pulling your energy inwards.

Five ♡

Don't get lost in the external world

It's crazy out there, but light up that craziness within you.

We all have a special uniqueness that we bring to this world. Whether it's your quirky personality, your sense of humour, your friendliness and/or your other quirky traits. We're all special with something unique to offer. When we lose sight of this it's very easy to get lost in the external world. With social media being the most used platform on our phones, it's easy to click onto Insta and see the life people are living through photos, or Tiktok where people create different types of videos. When consuming all the curated content from these talented, funny, intelligent, successful strangers it can become easy to forget what we bring to this world when we're consumed by what we see.

Existing in the external world looks like enjoying moments such as: going for a walk along the beach, enjoying eating ice cream and chocolate, it's where we get to go on adventures and explore nature, it's going out for dinner, it's where we have relationships that we are present for. There are so many fun things we can do in the external world that bring us joy and happiness, and there's also times where we may start to feel like we're getting lost and losing a sense of hope of who we are that we start feeling overwhelmed. When we begin to feel this way and not sure why, it's best to start with bringing awareness to it, acknowledging it, questioning it, and finding out why you are feeling that way.

These days we have so many external influences that it can be easy to lose ourselves. We become consumed by events or by anything that we're addicted too, it may be social media, being on our phones, the demands of our manager, the expectations of our jobs, or someone who constantly shops online. Getting lost can happen through any addiction. You become so focused on something outside of you that you become consumed by it. In this state it is easy for someone to forget who they are, they forget what they enjoy doing, they forget to just be…to just be present in the moment, to just be them. It's common for a lot of people to have the expectation that they 'need to be a certain type of person' but they forget to be the person they already are. If you were driven by parent expectations, or by looking at your peers, it's quite easy to get lost in that, as that's all you've grown up with or have been focusing on. And just as I'll share in my story, I had a tunnel vision lens on, and I could feel the heaviness on my mental health.

When I was 17 years old, I initially only had one Instagram page that had 17,000 followers, I ended up deleting it because I got lost in it spending hours trying to get the 'perfect shot', hours trying to find the 'right filter'. It was getting to the point where I consumed ALL my time on Instagram. I wasn't present when I was spending time with family and I made myself look a certain way when I knew it wasn't me. For those that know me, I don't really wear make-up and if I do it's for an event or if I'm going out to dinner. And every time I would take photos for my Instagram page, I made sure I had make-up on, did my hair and would do everything to look as best as I could. The reason why I spent many hours taking photos was because I never liked the way the photos turned out, even if it was the slightest thing such as the position of my hand or finger. It was the smallest details that would bother me because every time I discovered another girl's page they looked 'perfect', all their photos were 'on point', I couldn't fault them and I wanted to be the same. Though one day it got to a point where I realised that it wasn't healthy and I deleted my page. A few days later I made a brand new Instagram page and over time it grew up to have 20,000 followers. Yet again I deleted it for the same reasons above. I was becoming way too consumed on the app and it started to bother me because nothing was ever 'good enough'.

I could never take the right photo and could never find the right filter. I even started to stress if the photo I was going to post would look good next to the photo last posted on my page. It's safe to say I was and am glad that I realised it wasn't healthy and I couldn't keep going on like this over Instagram, over PHOTOS!

Don't get me wrong, I love photography, I love scenic photos, family photos, pet photos, all different types of photos. But being addicted to photos on Instagram was just not healthy. I once again deleted that 20,000-followers-Instagram page and made a promise to myself that if I was to create another page, I wouldn't get so caught up in it. I must say it wasn't easy when I jumped back on, but I definitely wasn't in that mindset of everything needing to be 'perfect' because of what I was seeing on other people's pages. Jumping back onto Instagram now and having 720 followers, I feel more at ease as I don't have the external pressure of having "a lot of followers." If anything, I find that I now have more engaging followers that share the same interest as me and I post photos, quotes, or videos that I'm interested in. This is also important as what we watch, see, and hear consumes our energy, and remember your energy is precious.

I one day decided to switch off my Instagram notifications so I could no longer see when someone likes my photo or is requesting to follow me. And from doing that it allowed me to not look at my phone so frequently and allowed me to be more present throughout my day. It took time to adjust to at the start but then over time it became the new normal for me, that I even decided to turn off my snapchat notifications. From that little tweak I created a healthy relationship with my phone use and social media. Now on Instagram I just go with the flow, I love my photos, I love capturing the moment, I love making memories, I love editing them, I love making everything suit, but I don't stress about it, I don't worry about when I'll post a photo or stress if I look 100% okay, I just let it be for what it is and I love it because everything now flows with less stress.

The moral of my social media story is that when we get caught up in trying to 'look' and 'be' a certain way it usually doesn't work out for us because we're not authentically happy, we're only doing it to look good. Be and do you and I promise you everything will flow, there may be a transition period but trust that everything will smooth out.

When we get lost in the external world we lose sight of who we are, and can lose touch with what our values and morals are, so we begin to look for validation in our external world with a restricted tunnel vision lens on. We can become so influenced and affected by what we see on social media, that we start to compare ourselves with the highlight reel of those we see on Instagram, TikTok, or Snapchat. From this our self-esteem lowers, our self-worth becomes non-existence, we begin to feel jealous, frustrated, feel a sense of hopelessness, but can also become judgemental and begin to resent those around us. We begin to focus our valuable energy on other people's lives rather than our own, we even begin to have disrupted sleep as we constantly think of what and how other people are living their life and how we can be like them. A lack of sleep leads to a lack of begin able to focus on our day-to-day routine.

When you're looking for who you are in the external world, you're looking for permission to be who you are.

Read that again.

You're looking for validation from your external world. And while this may feel great for a short period of time receiving validations from others, it's only temporary and we can't have it all the time. This then means you won't be able to live the life you want to create, you won't be able to have the relationships you want, enjoy your work and be your authentic self because your happiness is coming from your external world.

When we're so focused on the external world it's only natural to compare yourself to someone else as that's where our attention is. However, when we're lost in the external world and we're searching for things to make us feel good, there comes a point where there's only so many things we can focus on. And while it's amazing that getting lost can lead us to adventure, when we bring awareness to turn our gaze back into our internal world, we realise how we can turn those adventures inwards and the magic we can discover and explore within getting to know ourselves.

Would you allow your child self to feel the way you do when you are addicted to distractions or lost? Would you allow your child self to feel the frustration, purposelessness, and struggle that often comes with getting lost in the external world? Imagine your child self standing in front of you right now as you answer these questions.

This is not to say social media only impacts us negatively. Social media has both positive and negative effects and it's the perception we have towards it that determines how we allow it to make us feel. It's okay if you have fallen into these traps, it's so common, however, once you have this awareness you then get to choose how you want to live your life and where you focus your time and energy.

Once we have that awareness of turning in and searching for adventure within, we begin to find who we are, our morals and values and our self-worth. We learn how to exist in the external world without getting lost in it by being influenced by social media or friends and we know how to still be our authentic self. This may look like you taking photos of you and friends while you're all dressed up wearing nice formal clothes and you realise your body position isn't the way you want it to be but all your friends are standing the same way. Knowing that you all look great including yourself and still wanting to post it to social media because you know that you look great, you're happy with who you are, and you know you don't need to compare yourself to others. Life becomes stress free and you're able to exist in a world full of differences and still shine bright.

Key points:

- Enjoy the moments you experience. The moments where you set your inner child free, where you're surrounded by loved ones and most importantly the moments where you feel more than yourself than ever before.

- Don't get lost in the external world.

- Don't get lost in social media.

- Don't get lost in what you see on TV.

- Don't get lost in other people's appearance.

- Don't get lost in allowing other people to create your happiness.

- You are already complete.

- When you know who you are, your morals, your values, your mission, what your strengths and weaknesses are, and what makes you happy your authentic self will shine through.

You don't need **permission** and **validation** to be who you already are.

"To change our state of being, we have to change how we think and feel." – Dr. Joe Dispenza

Six ♡
The happy self

By now, you would have realised that you're in control of your life, the decisions you make, how you feel during a situation, and the environments you're in. It's now time to combine it all together and create the happy ending for this journey becoming yourself.

This is the exciting part; as this is taking everything you've learnt and putting it into action. Knowing that you're going to have some good days and you're going to ride that high, but you're also going to have some not so good days and that's okay too. It's all a part of your journey into becoming the best version of you, and you and I know that no one can do that but YOU!

Appreciate all the little things that you accomplish every day that leads you to exactly where you want to be, embrace all the emotions you've experienced throughout the day and release them, remove your own barriers to your happiness. Dr. Joe Dispenza says "your thoughts are incredibly powerful, choose yours wisely."

Start looking inwards and discover the happiness from within you.

Start checking in on yourself regularly and ask yourself 'how am I feeling today?'.

Begin building on your self-esteem by thinking about how you would treat your inner child.

Allow yourself to be vulnerable, allow yourself to present and take the time to appreciate everything you are doing for yourself every day, as this takes time and work.

You are the only one who can give yourself permission to be who you are and you don't need anyone else to prove that. I wrote this book as reading and writing have always been a passion of mine since I can remember, and I've always felt the desire to share my voice. I've used my passion to create a book, a book that may change your perspective on your own experiences throughout life. And throughout this journey no one gave me permission but myself to become an author, to become something I've always wanted to be. In times where self-doubt and over thinking start to rain on you, just remember you're in control and no one can change that but *you*.

Becoming your authentic self will look different for everyone. I've shared parts of my journey with you; your journey may be similar or may be completely different. While you go through the process of discovering who you are, just remember all you have to do is; *be you*.

When you become the person you truly are, you're able to experience life in a different light, you're able to understand that challenges will still arise as that's a part of life, but you're able to work through those challenges with a different mindset, with an understanding of knowing that you don't need to relate to every person, you just have to be aware and listen, as awareness is a state of presence. You're able to feel a sense of joy knowing you know your values, morals, strengths, and weaknesses. When you realise you are no longer trapped in the conditioning of who you thought you were, you'll be able to connect with life in a conscious light.

On Sunday the 26th of March 2023, as I was finalising my writing for this book, I was fortunate enough to see the man who taught me how to present, speak on stage, the man who is the author of the first book I read to awaken my spiritual practice- Eckhart Tolle. It was quite interesting as everything I took away from the two hours spent in the room with him, is just about everything that sums up this chapter. A really great example he mentioned during his talk that has stuck with me and will stick with me is; as we're conditioned from our upbringing and growing up as adults, some of us still live the conditioned life, this is like living life from a script. You have this script that is created for you, which is you as a child growing up and learning different ways on how to do things, and so you follow this script and play it out and from doing so you begin to create this identity for yourself. You begin to create this person that doesn't feel like they're worthy enough because that's how they were treated as a child, you don't give yourself the opportunity to become the person you really are. To become the girl stripped back from her conditionings as a child, that is able to create the person she wants to be.

Awakening, and discovering who you are to the core, almost never happens in your comfort zone. Some people may pick up Eckhart Tolle's book and put it back on the shelf feeling like they don't need it and seven years later they may pick the same book back up again from the same spot and something happens to them as they begin to read it, they slowly start to awaken. As you go on your own journey of awakening, you'll start to become present and when you become present you start to realise there's no thinking as you're in the moment and watch how no other thought will cross your mind.

Creating your happy self is an ongoing journey that has no end date. As Eckhart Tolle said during his two-hour seminar "time really isn't there, we label it and make us think we need time, but really we don't. You can reach the end of the time of what you're doing and still feel and be the same." Let that sink in.

Trust that your journey is exactly what you need to experience to discover who you are and become the best version of you. And as you go on through your journey if you feel you relapse just remember that it's okay, use the tools you learnt to get to where you know you can be and stay consistent. Show up for yourself every damn day. That can look like waking up and not being on your phone for fifteen minutes and each day you begin to adapt to not being on your phone for fifteen minutes. As the days, weeks, and months go on you build yourself up to not being on your phone for half an hour, forty-five minutes and it just continues to get longer and longer so you have the space to go inwards and reconnect to who you are and who you want to be at the beginning of every day.

One last thing, before you finish this book and be the baddest bi$tch you've ever been, just remember that you will become a better person when you're no longer feeding your ego and when your ego no longer controls your thoughts and action.

Key points:

Journal prompts to support with reflecting on each day:

- What was my favourite thing about today?
- What are three things I'm grateful for about today?
- How did you stay true to yourself today?
- How can I make tomorrow better?
- Don't forget "your thoughts are incredibly powerful, choose yours wisely" – Dr. Joe Dispenza

This is where the work gets done. This is where you discover who you are and create your happy self. Remember no one can create your happy self but you.

You're in **control** and you've **got this**!

As this book comes to an end,

I want you to think about and write down three to five things that have crossed your mind since reading this book, and I want you to slowly start making a change to your daily routine, to your life that will lead you **becoming yourself through the noise.**

_____

_____

_____

_____

_____

_____

_____

_____

_____

_____

_____

_____

With Thanks ♡

Writing a book using my own personal experiences was a great reflection on how much growth I have had in the last four years. Growth takes time so don't put any pressure or a timeline on yourself to be a certain way before a certain time.

Trust in the process, trust in the journey, trust that the universe is guiding you and you are exactly where you need to be. Even when you're experiencing the highs and the lows, every moment is meant to be for you to experience and it's how we handle ourselves throughout the journey that the true growth comes from.

It's learning to love yourself through all different emotions and feelings and as long as you stay true to yourself, everything else will all flow naturally into place.

Thank you from the bottom of my heart for not only purchasing this book, but for taking the time out of your day to read this. I truly hope that you have either learnt something new or taken away something that you will work on within you. Just remember; you are so capable of achieving anything you want to, you just have to go out and do it.

With lots of love,

From Melissa.

REFERENCES

Breaking the Habit of Being Yourself [book] - Dr. Joe Dispenza.

The Power of Now [book]- Eckhart Tolle.

Flourishing in the first five years- Connecting Implications from Mind, Brain and Education Research to the Development of Young Children- Donna Wilson and Marcus Conyers.

https://www.amazon.com/Flourishing-First-Five-Years-Implications/dp/1475803184

ACKNOWLEDGEMENTS

To my wonderful mother Aliye, thank you for never giving up on me while growing up. Thank you for ensuring I had a roof over my head, for supporting me to keep pursuing my studies, and for always being a shoulder to cry on. Thank you for everything you've taught me and for never doubting me. I truly couldn't have done it without you. Love from your little angel.

To my dad Martin, I am so grateful that I still get to spend time with you. Love you always from your youngest daughter.

To my brother Hasim, thank you for always providing me with ample advice while in the process of birthing this book. You always were, and always are there for me when I need advice. You and I know how much our childhood has played a part in both of our lives now as adults and I know that whatever challenges we face, we will always get through it. Love you always, your baby sister.

To my sister Tamara, thank you for all your support and advice when needed to bring this book to life. I really can't thank you enough for being the big sister I needed as an adult. I know this book will play a massive part in your growth within your life now. Love you always, your baby sister.

To my brother Aron, thank you for always being so supportive and open to listening to everything I've wanted to share with you about this book. Your support and praise kept me going and you are part of the reason I'm so excited this book has been brought to life. Love you always, your support person.

To the universe, thank you for always having my back. You truly make me feel like no other, you know how to show up in ways I would never imagine, but those subtle little hints are what have kept me on track. I fricken love you.

To my partner Jacob, thank you for unintentionally reminding me to be the best version of myself. You're always reminding me to put myself first and do things that work best for me, no one else. You've taught me how to not settle for anything less in a partner. I love you so much.

To my mentor Rachel, thank you for being so patient, efficient, and helpful. Your support and guidance has helped allow me to bring this book together and I couldn't have done it without you. Thank you.

ABOUT THE AUTHOR

Melissa Mifsud is a qualified Early Childhood Teacher with the passion to lift, guide, and support those around her. Melissa expresses her creativity through reading, writing, or engaging in arts and crafts.

Melissa is a bubbly and friendly lady that always has a smile on her face and will cheer up those around her. Melissa deeply cares about her loved ones and will always do her best to ensure she helps those around her who she keeps close to her heart.

Melissa would love to connect with those who have read this book and would love to share some words, feedback, or even thoughts. Melissa is an open book and values people's feedback. You can connect with her on Instagram @melissamifsudx or via email on Melissa.mifsud@outlook.com

www.ingramcontent.com/pod-product-compliance
Lightning Source LLC
Chambersburg PA
CBHW020326010526
44107CB00054B/1991